Angels
to Watch Over Me

$\mathcal{A}$ngels
to Watch Over Me

What are Angels, how they can help, and
how to trust your own very special
Guardian Angel

Joanna Crosse

ELEMENT
CHILDREN'S BOOKS

SHAFTESBURY, DORSET · BOSTON, MASSACHUSETTS · MELBOURNE, VICTORIA

To all the angels who helped co-create this book!

© Element Children's Books 1998
Text © Joanna Crosse 1998
Illustrations © Paddy Mounter 1998

First published in the UK in 1998 by Element Children's Books
Shaftesbury, Dorset SP7 8BP

Published in the USA in 1999 by Element Books, Inc.
160 North Washington Street, Boston, MA 02114

Published in Australia in 1999 by Element Books and distributed by
Penguin Australia Ltd, 487 Maroondah Highway,
Ringwood, Victoria 3134

British Library Cataloguing in Publication data available.
Library of Congress Cataloging in Publication data available.

ISBN 1 901881 04 0

Cover design by Alison Withey
Cover illustration © Bee Willey 1998
Text design by Dorchester Typesetting Group Ltd
Printed in Hong Kong through World Print Ltd

Contents

Introduction

What is it about angels that captivates us all? Since time began, people have been fascinated by these bright, shining, winged messengers. Perhaps it's because they symbolize light and hope for us, especially in difficult times and situations.

Many children have seen and met angels, and some have even talked with their own personal guardian angel. There are also accounts of children being rescued by so-called humans who disappear into thin air after they've completed their mission. And what about the "invisible friends" so many of us played with when we were little? Adults often dismiss them as figments of the imagination, but that doesn't mean they don't exist – it's just that some people see angels more easily than others.

Many children, especially older ones, say that they think angels are what you want them to be. And it's true that angels appear to us in the form we believe they should take. So, if you imagine that angels have multicolored wings and wear white gowns, that's probably how an angel would appear to you. Some people describe them as dots of light, colored spheres, or even clouds in the sky. It really doesn't matter what form your angel takes – it's your contact with the angelic realm that counts.

It might be nice just to say that all angels are goodness and light, and leave it at that. But that isn't the case. There are what are known as fallen angels, or demons. But they are definitely in the minority. A way to make the idea of demons a little less scary is to think of the good angels as the best part of ourselves, and the little imps as the naughty part. After all, you cannot have light without darkness, or there would be no balance in the world.

The mischievous angels are the ones who might encourage us to sneak a look at someone else's paper when we're stuck for an answer on a math exam, or grab a few chocolates when we've been told, "No snacks before dinner." The angels of light and love will point out what's best for us and others in any situation, whereas the naughty angels will tell us that the only thing that's important is looking out for number one. But sticking with the good angels brings you bigger bonuses every time!

It's important to remember that there are trillions more good angels than bad ones, and that they are here to help us. These special spiritual messengers are sent to accompany each of us on our journey through life, helping us love one another and the earth we live on. All we need to do is remember they're there, and call on them.

8

chapter 1

What Are Angels?

Angels are whatever you think they are. It's said that our celestial friends often appear to humans in the way we expect them to. For example, if you imagine an angel to be dressed in wonderful, colorful robes, with wings of burning gold, then that's probably what you're going to see.

For many of us, angels stay in the invisible realms. We may be more likely to see them in times of need, in our dreams, or when we deliberately try to contact them. But don't worry if you can't see them at all. Some of us are more kinesthetic than visual – in other words, we feel or sense things rather than see them.

Some say they can smell the perfume of angels, or even feel wings on their back. These are all signs that there's lots of help around, even if it's not

9

always obvious. Each one of us on earth has our very own guardian angel assigned to us at birth, and it's that angel's job to keep a watchful eye on us throughout every day and night of our life.

It's wonderful to know there's that extra help for us to rely on, but lots of people aren't aware of this amazing guiding force in their lives. They don't realize that their every earthly wish and desire is being heard – but it is.

Angels Everywhere

"Angel" comes from the Greek word *angelos,* meaning "messenger," but angels are known by other names, too. One of those is *malakh,* which is Hebrew for "messenger." *Deva* is a Sanskrit word that means "shining one." It doesn't matter what we call them, their purpose is the same – to bring light and love to the planet, and to act as the link between the visible and invisible worlds.

And guess what – there is an angel for absolutely everything. It's even said that every blade of grass on the planet has its own guardian angel to help it grow! There are angels for people, animals, places, countries. And there are special angels assigned to help us learn to love ourselves, others, and Mother Earth.

Help, Not Interference

The most important thing to remember about the angels is that although they are more than willing to help us on our journey, they will never *ever* interfere in anything we do unless we specifically ask them to.

One of the most important aspects of being human is that we have free will, which means we can decide how to behave, think, and feel. The angels, of course, know this, and recognize that we are all meant to use our free will.

They can be our guiding light and our source of comfort or connection to the power of creation, but because they respect our humanness they will never deliberately interfere or even try to help us out unless we call on them to do so – except in a dire emergency.

Emergency Aid

There are times when we need more than a gentle message from the angels, and that's when they can step in to help. They can break a dangerous fall, push us out of the way of oncoming cars, and perform what may seem like a miracle in order to save a life.

One woman described how she and her baby daughter were thrown from their car after it was involved in an accident. But she felt a hand literally scooping them up and putting them gently on the ground, so neither of them was seriously hurt.

Friends in Need

It's said that we can be helped by an angel and not even know it. When they have to be visible in order to help us out of a serious situation, angels may come in disguise.

There are many stories about people's experiences with these heavenly beings. People have told, for instance, how they've been rescued by strangers who seem to disappear into thin air once they've carried out their angelic duty.

One of those stories tells of a ten-year-old girl who was rowing onto a lake as night was approaching. She became very frightened as the sky turned pitch black and she realized the lake was even bigger than she had thought it was. Just as she was wondering how she would ever get back to shore, a shadowy figure appeared in the distance, holding a lamp. He beckoned the girl to row toward him. When she finally got safely to the water's edge, the person seemed to vanish into thin air.

If this ever happens to you – if you're ever helped out of a crisis by someone you've never seen before, and never meet again – it just might be an encounter with an angel.

> *"Be not forgetful to entertain strangers: for thereby some have entertained angels unawares."*
>
> (Hebrews: 13:2)

~ ~ Angel Thoughts ~ ~

"An angel is a small white bird with wings. It grants wishes to help people and eats funny food."

Matthew, age 8

"An angel has long hair if it is a girl and short if it's a boy. They have long, shaped wings and a very beautiful face, and clothing in all different colors."

Rebecca, age 11

✦ ✦ ✦
chapter 2

Types of Angels

As we've said, there's a guardian angel for every living thing on earth, every member of the animal, mineral, and plant kingdom. But these angels aren't flying randomly all over the place. Angels have a specific order, just as people have structured societies here on earth. Some angels work very closely with the Creator, and others work under them, doing a whole range of specific jobs.

The Angelic Orders
There are nine angelic orders, or choirs:

> *SERAPHIM • CHERUBIM • THRONES*
> *DOMINATIONS • VIRTUES • POWERS*
> *PRINCIPALITIES • ARCHANGELS • ANGELS*

The higher an angel's rank, the more wings it has. The *Seraphim*, whose name means "warmth," and whose job is looking after love, have six wings each – two for covering the face, two over the feet, and two that are used for flying. Their leader is Uriel.

The *Cherubim* are in charge of wisdom, and they have four wings each. Jophiel is the leader of the Cherubim.

The *Thrones* are called that because they are said to be God's throne bearers. They're seen as very majestic and divine, and their leader is Japhkiel.

The *Dominations* carry a sword and a scepter, the symbols of power. Led by Zadkiel, they look after the power of creation.

The *Virtues* are led by Janiel and look after the will of God. They bear the message of unconditional love and forgiveness.

The *Powers* carry flaming swords, to symbolize their role as protectors of humans. Their leader is Raphael.

The *Principalities* are led by Chamel. Along with the *Archangels,* and *Angels,* the Principalities work closely with the physical world.

Let's look at some of the main Archangels in more detail, because it's useful to know who to call on in times of need!

14

The Archangels

Archangels are the leaders of groups of angels, who are the ninth choir and are the ones we may be most familiar with.

Michael is the chief Archangel, and his name, which means "Who is like God," is said to be his battle cry. He is here to protect us, and he is often pictured with a flaming sword in his hand to represent his battle with Satan. In other words, he's here to slay the demons, and that's why he is often called on to help clear up negative situations. Archangel Michael is linked with the sun and the element of fire, and he's a great one to connect with if you want some courage! His season is autumn.

Archangel Raphael is the angel of healing, and in fact his name means "healing" in Hebrew. Often shown with a snake, he guards the Tree of Life in the Garden of Eden. He's also believed to watch over people on earth, especially in hospitals and doctors' offices. Raphael is also very involved with communication. His season is spring.

Archangel Gabriel is best known as the one who told Mary that she was going to have a baby boy who would save the world. The name Gabriel means "God's strength." He's a messenger, a bringer of good news and messages of love, and he watches over Paradise. He is said to be the ruler of the moon, and his season is winter.

15

Metatron is the tallest angel and is a symbol of truth and purpose. He's sometimes known as the king of the angels, and he is said to stand at the top of the Tree of Life, which is the link between heaven and earth.

Uriel's name means "God's fire" in Hebrew, and he's the angel of creativity, the one who "fires up" artists, writers, and musicians with inspiration. In fact, he can inspire anyone who has goals to achieve. He is associated with summer.

Haniel is the angel of love. If you ever have an argument with someone you love, Haniel is definitely the angel to call on to heal things and help you make up!

Raziel is the angel of mysteries and knowledge and is pretty hot on the ideas front. Call on him if you need help with new ideas and concepts.

Auriel is a night angel, and connected with Mother Earth. He's a good angel to make contact with if you want to think more deeply about something.

Our Own Angels

The archangels are there for all of us, but we mustn't forget about our very own personal angels. Each one of us has a special angel who's given to us at birth and who is with us throughout this life on earth. In addition, we can also invite many other angels to support us at different stages of our lives, or when we're faced with various challenges.

Don't imagine that just because you might not be able to see, hear, or feel your angel that this special helper is far away. It is quite possible to have a close relationship with your celestial friend – and here's one way to do it.

16

Angel Exercise

First of all, find a quiet place where you're not likely to be disturbed.

Sit comfortably, close your eyes, and take a few deep breaths so you feel really relaxed. Now, all you have to do is call in your guardian angel.

Imagine in your mind's eye meeting your angel for the first time. You could start by asking its name, and just seeing what comes up. You may not hear a voice, but a name might just pop into your head.

When you've got the name, welcome your angel. Then try starting a conversation. You may be amazed at the messages you receive!

If there's anything troubling you, no matter how small, ask your angel to take the worry away.

Remember, it doesn't matter what you see – it might be specks of light, flashes of color, or a beautiful vision of a winged being. Whatever you see, it's your own personal connection to the angelic realm. Each of us has a unique, personal way of knowing and meeting with our guardian angel. It's just great to know that help is always close by.

~ ~ Angel Thoughts ~ ~

"Angels have little white hats. They are on computers. They are a bit stupid. They are daddy's girls. They are very funny."

Daniel, age 8

"Angels – they light up!"

Cassie, age 8

chapter 3

Personal Guardian Angels

Your guardian angel is like your personal protector. This guide will see you into the world, accompany you on your journey through life, and will even be there to help you move from this life into whatever awaits us afterward. Although you can pick up a few more angels along the way, this one special being is *always* at your side, day and night.

It can be quite magical to discover that you have this support. An angel can soothe your tears, ease your fears, and share the funnier, lighter moments in your life – not to mention the celebrations! The more you communicate with your angel, the more you will find you are able to develop a close and ongoing relationship.

An Angel Prayer

Throughout history, many different cultures, religions, and faith systems all over the world have held strong beliefs in angels. This is a lovely prayer* that some children have been taught to say:

Angel of God, my guardian dear
To whom His love commits me here
Ever this day or night; be at my side
To light and guard, to rule and guide.

Angel Communications

One of the main ways your angel will talk to you is through your intuition, or what's sometimes called the sixth sense. This is the inner alarm bell that goes off if you're in any danger; it also gives you positive messages to tell you when you're on the right track and that all's well. These messages could be said to come from the higher part of yourself, which can take a kind of overview and warn you about what's coming next – or they could be coming from your guardian angel.

A Link to Heaven

Our guardian angel is our bridge to the heavenly world, or the realms where love, peace, and tolerance exist. We all have times in our lives when it's hard

*A Catholic prayer, from *Messengers of Light* by Terry Lynn Taylor (H. J. Kramer, 1990).

to be loving, kind, and forgiving – and those may be the times we need our angel most. It's our angel's job to remind us that we are bright, light souls who need to love and be loved more than anything else on earth.

So if you're feeling down and a little sorry for yourself, just remember to call on your invisible friend for a cheer-up session. You have nothing but happiness to gain!

Seeing the Light

Angels may be invisible friends to most of us, but some people have seen their angels. This is what ten-year-old Amy said:

"I was snuggling down in my bed, all ready to go to sleep. Then suddenly I saw a bright light – it was blinding. At first it was blurry, but then it came clearer. I realized then it was an angel. I felt it sit on my bed, and it said:

'One day you will be with me.'
Then I said in my mind, 'Yes.'

I felt an overwhelming deep joy and warmth in my heart. Then the angel got up and faded away. I felt very peaceful and fell asleep. This happened when I was seven."

~ ~ Angel Thoughts ~ ~

"An angel is something from heaven – God's messenger. A guardian angel is someone who protects you."

Traian, age 11

"Angels have wings and a sort of dress on, and a halo, and they give me great big happiness."

Emily, age 4

⬦ ⬦ ⬦

chapter 4

Children and Angels

hen we look at the hierarchy of angels we see that there are lots of different celestial departments, which is a good thing – without all that organization, things would get very chaotic! One of the most important departments is the one for the guardian angels of children.

As you know, each one of us has our very own personal guardian angel who keeps watch over us. They're there all our lives, but they keep an extra-special eye out for us in the early stages of our life, to help keep us out of trouble and to help us hold on to our innocence and love of creation.

Talking to Angels

Have you ever noticed how babies and small children can appear to be having an animated conversation, or a lively giggling and gurgling session, when there doesn't seem to be anyone else around? Some people say that's when they're communicating with the angels.

Infants and small children are very open to experiences of the angelic realms, because they haven't been around long enough to learn what so many adults believe – that their celestial visions are all in their imagination!

Angels on the Rooftop

Ronne remembers seeing angels when she was seven years old. *"It was dark, and I was in bed. I looked out the window and saw three figures, the size of children, that seemed to be made of light. They were hovering over the roof of the house across the street. I was very excited, because I knew they were angels, and I called my mother to show her. But by the time she got to my room, they had disappeared. She said it was probably just my imagination, and told me to go to sleep – but years later, she told me she'd been thinking about the incident, and now believed I may have seen angels after all. I've never doubted it!"*

Heavenly Protectors

Because kids are naturally curious and adventurous, and love to go exploring, they sometimes need a winged friend or two to look out for them. Sometimes, in an emergency, these invisible friends might even appear fleetingly in human form.

In fact, more and more people are saying that they've encountered angels like these. There are an increasing number of books on the market that tell stories of miraculous rescues made by angels with no trace of wings or halos. They're just mysterious people who seem to appear from nowhere exactly when they're needed, and who disappear into thin air once they've completed their mission.

Imaginary Friends?

It's often said that angels will appear to children as children, because it's easier for a child to relate to someone of his or her own age. Lots of small children talk about their invisible friends, and it may well be that the "imaginary playmate" is that child's personal guardian angel.

Meg says that the first time she became aware of angels was when she was just three years old. She says she was sitting at the dinner table next to her father when she noticed three round, white faces by her side. She says she just knew they were angels. After that they became regular companions at the table!

A Bridge Between Worlds

Angels are very eager to communicate with us humans, but because we've been given free will, it is completely up to us to invite them into our lives.

Imagine that there's a bridge between this world and the invisible realms. The angels are on the other side of this bridge, working very hard to help make our planet a better place. But there's nothing like teamwork to get a job done well, and if we start joining in more on this side, then more will get done.

Those Who've Departed

It's said that children who die young are special souls who have only a short mission here on earth this time around. Some people believe that when children die they turn into angels and watch over the loved ones they've left behind on earth.

Here's a true story, told by ten-year-old Chloe: *"After my cousin died her mother, who's my auntie, saw her as an angel. She appeared with another angelic friend and she was bright and shining and was sort of gold in color."*

~ ~ *Angel Thoughts* ~ ~

"An angel looks like a fairy. She is white with wings. They sing songs and take care of you."

Ross, age 5

"An angel came to Mary to say she was going to have a baby. The angels on TV have halos on their head. There are angels in heaven, and they wear white a lot."

Vicky, age 8

just a decorative header of stars

✧ ✧ ✧

chapter 5

Angels of Love

*I*t's said that the Seraphim, who are the highest angelic order, are the angels who carry the message of love on their wings. In a sense they are the guardian angels of love for all of creation.

The Many Forms of Love

We've all experienced love of some kind in our lives, whether it's the feelings we have for our families, or the doting love of a parent, or, as we grow up, the kind of love we share in partnerships or marriage. Love comes in many forms and can be shown in many different ways – through words, hugs, gifts, or even just through doing something for someone else.

A Special Kind of Love

Unconditional love literally means love without conditions. This special kind of love, which doesn't ask for anything in

27

return, is said to be the foundation stone for life, indeed for the whole universe. Most parents would say they love their children unconditionally – in other words, it doesn't matter what their kids do, no matter how bad it may seem, their parents still love them.

When you love unconditionally, you can forgive someone no matter how badly your feelings may have been hurt. If you love someone this way, you don't judge them by what they do, you just love them for who they are.

This kind of love can be hard for human beings to feel. We all have needs to be met, and just to love someone without reward sometimes seems impossible. But this is the love the angels give us.

The Power to Heal

It can be hard to feel love all the time, especially living in a world that contains sadness, pain, and loss as well as love, joy, and happiness. But the power of love knows no bounds. It is the creative energy of the universe and can transform all living things. It is a miracle worker, and some people believe it is the ultimate answer to all our personal and worldly problems. It can heal and comfort and help us to be tolerant, patient, and kind. Having a loving and open heart also makes us feel great!

The angels of love include the Archangel Raphael and the Roman goddess Venus, who's considered by some people to be an angel. Raphael is also the angel of healing, which is exactly what love does. Just think about how good you feel when someone shows how much they love you and care for you.

Giving love as well as receiving it can fill us with a nice warm glow, and somehow the energy of love makes the world seem a brighter and happier place. If you're ever feeling down in the dumps, ask the angels of love to shine their bright rays of warmth on you, and you can bet they'll appear to you in some form or another. Just calling in the angels of love will help push away any worries, fears, or resentments you have and make you feel a whole lot better.

Angel Exercise

What do you think love feels like, sounds like, or looks like? For some people it might be a fluffy cloud, for others a beautiful landscape, or it might come as the sound of violins or the waves of the sea.

Close your eyes and ask your angels to show you something that represents love. Maybe it's stroking a puppy, or maybe it's a walk in beautiful countryside, or it might be just being with the people you love most. It really doesn't matter, as long as it helps you get in touch with that feeling of love.

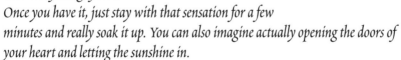

Once you have it, just stay with that sensation for a few minutes and really soak it up. You can also imagine actually opening the doors of your heart and letting the sunshine in.

Allow yourself to stay with this wonderful feeling for a while, and then, when you're ready, come back to the present moment. Then you can take that feel-good factor out there into your life.

Love in Action

"Love in action" is a phrase that delights the angels. It means showing your love by *doing*. Running an errand for your neighbor, helping someone in your family, or taking the time to say a few comforting words to a friend who's feeling blue will not only be a great gift for the people you help, but it will do wonders for you too.

All love begins with being able to love yourself. The better you feel about yourself, the more likely you are to feel good about others. If you find yourself feeling a bit unloved, try the exercise on the previous page. You'll be amazed at how wonderful it can make you feel.

~ ~ *Angel Thoughts* ~ ~

"An angel is a lady with a dress, wings, a hoop on her head, and a magic wand. One thing angels do is collect teeth."

Keiran, age 8

"I think angels come into this world to help us learn. Sometimes they look like people and their wings have been sawn off."

Alicia, age 5

chapter 6

Angels of Happiness

Wouldn't life be great if we could feel happy all the time? Well, on second thought, maybe not. If we felt happy all the time, we'd forget what it was like to feel unhappy, and after a while we'd take that wonderful warm glow for granted and wouldn't be able to appreciate it.

Well, for better or worse, most of us don't feel happy all the time, and when we're miserable, all we want is to feel better. Luckily, there are a host of angels all over the universe whose task it is to create happiness. Some people might call that creating heaven on earth in the form of blessings.

The Best in Everything

Different blessings make different people feel happy. What does happiness mean to you? Try writing a list of all the events or material things that make you feel good. Then take a look at that list and ask yourself if any of those things would bring you long-term happiness. The thrill of a new computer game or pair of rollerblades might bring temporary joy, but it's really how we feel on the inside that brings us true happiness.

Happiness also depends on how we see our lives. In a sense, this is the essence of the angels – seeing the best in everything, and feeling love and joy as a result.

For example, the happiness angels would encourage us to make the best of what may look like a bad situation. So instead of getting upset because it's raining, the angels would encourage you to get creative and do all the indoor things that you don't get a chance to do when the sun's shining. The happiness angels' message would be, "Don't focus on the weeds, look at the beautiful flowers!"

Happy All the Time?

Of course, it's unrealistic to expect to be happy all the time, and we can't appreciate happiness unless we've experienced sadness or loss. But the angels of happiness help us to see how we can change our attitudes. Their message is that true happiness is not dependent on what's happening in our lives – it's about how we respond to particular situations and to our life in general. Do we feel blessed or bereft? Is life a tragedy or a comedy? Is it a disaster or a great learning experience?

The happiness angels can teach us to see how a negative situation may help us change in a positive way – so that we can feel good about our lives and ourselves, even on the rainiest day.

Catch the Happiness Bug!

Have you ever noticed how being around someone who's bright and bubbly makes you start feeling the same way? Happiness is infectious, and the more you get in touch with it the more you're likely to feel it.

Try and apply this idea to even the most boring situations in your life – think "happy"! For example, when you're told to go and clean up your room, start by imagining how happy you're going to feel when it's been done. Concentrate on enjoying the process of seeing your room transformed from a heap to organized shelves and clear floor space. The good feelings this will set off in you are bound to make the rest of your family feel happy, too – so happiness is definitely catching!

Positive thinking creates a state of happiness. Believe the best will happen and it will. Most important, ask the angels of happiness to fly a little closer and help you get in touch with those good feelings.

Feeling truly happy can help us do just about anything. It's like being given a head start – and once you're off and running, you'll be unstoppable!

~ ~ *Angel Thoughts* ~ ~

"Angels hopefully go to heaven. They're all dressed up, and look like fairies."

Jethro, age 8

"An angel is a bird, but it has a human's face and wings, and it looks after me."

Charlotte, age 7

chapter 7

Traveling with Angels

We're all on a journey through life, and there are angels to help us along every step of the way. But did you know that there are actually specific angels assigned to highways, flight paths, and ocean crossings?

Riding on Angels' Wings

It's comforting to know that every vehicle we ride in and every road we travel along has its own guardian angel. In fact, it's probably got a host of angels. St. Christopher is said to be the patron saint (or angel) of traveling, and he's often pictured crossing a river with his staff in hand, carrying a child on his back. Well in the same way, the angels are there to help us travel from one destination to another – we just have to remember they're there, even if we can't see them.

Some people say communicating with the guardian angel of the car or plane they're in really does give them a safe and wonderful feeling. Next time you board an airplane, just sit quietly in your seat for a moment, close your eyes, and ask the angel of that particular craft to look after all the passengers and crew and make sure they have a good flight.

Several people claim they've seen angels out of airplane windows. They may not have come complete with wings and a halo, but they may have appeared as clouds, or in another form that's obviously angelic.

Think about the waves on the ocean. Water can create the most magical patterns and forms, and some people say they've seen angels dancing on the surf. Billions of sparkling lights shimmer on the sea when the sunlight hits the water in particular ways. Perhaps those billions of lights are a connection to the angelic realm.

Don't Leave Home Without One!

We are literally surrounded by angels, but most of us either don't know it or don't remember it. But you need never leave home without an angel at your side! Next time you go on a journey, just call on your winged friends and check in with them. Knowing that there's an extra-special watchful eye looking over you will certainly help you feel protected and secure.

Here's something you can try for fun. This will definitely boost your belief in the angelic realm.

Angel Exercise

Believe it or not, there are angels of parking spaces!

Now, although you probably haven't spent much time, if any, behind the wheel of a car yet, you no doubt spend plenty of time encouraging your family and friends to give you lifts. So you've probably encountered the problem of parking spaces – or rather the lack of them. Well, next time you find yourself with someone who's in this predicament, just ask the angel of parking spaces to help you out. According to some people, this never fails! So if you can't quite believe it when that parking space magically appears, try it again another time and watch the same thing happen!

~ ~ Angel Thoughts ~ ~

"I have a guardian angel, and once I saw it. It had a very nice face and wings. Angels can help children to believe in a God, and to not do very bad things, and to be nicer."

Carrick, age 9

"I think everyone has their own guardian angel. I know mine helped me pass my exams to get into senior school."

Posy, age 11

✧✧✧

chapter 8

Life and Death

B y now you know that we each have a guardian angel who's with us from the moment we come into the world and who helps us to leave it when we move to another dimension – when we die.

As St. Augustine said: "Every visible thing in this world is put in the charge of an angel."

Coming into the World

It's said that angels are particularly close to children, from the moment of birth through the earliest days of their life. They give children a little more space as they get older, because we all have free will – the power to choose how to live our life – and that's something the angels respect and wouldn't dream of interfering with. It's important to stress, though, that even though the angels present at our birth

37

might give us a bit more room, they are never really far away. The minute we call on them, they fly straight in and support us!

Angels love children because of their natural joy in life, their happiness and spontaneity. The angels draw up a kind of blueprint at birth – of love, goodness, and kindness toward others – and it's their job to make sure those positive foundations are set down firmly and securely.

A Candle That Never Goes Out

Although our angels are here to help us into the world, and indeed to look after us during our lifetime, one of their missions is to help us understand what death means.

Naturally enough, for most of us the idea of death is frightening, and not something we necessarily want to look at. But the angels can help us see that dying is merely moving from one world to another – a little like moving from one room to another, or crossing a bridge to a new place. Or we can think of it as taking off the coat we've been wearing in this life so we can move into another dimension. We all have what's known as a light body, which is like a candle that never goes out. We can imagine that as being the invisible body under the coat we've chosen to wear for our life on earth.

Crossing the Bridge

Some people say they've actually seen an angel coming at the time of death

38

sensed the presence of a very large angel in the house, and just a couple of days later, without any prompting, Sedona said that she'd seen a huge angel in the house. She explained that it had appeared to her when she was in bed. With all the natural innocence of childhood, Sedona described the incident as if angels appear to everyone, at any time of day. Actually, they're probably there – it's just that we don't see them!

Can't you just imagine them, all perched on the rooftops, keeping guard? It's a wonderful thought. Who needs a burglar alarm when you can just ask the angel of the house to look after everything while you're away!

An Angelic Atmosphere

We all know about "atmosphere" – lots of people talk about the atmosphere of places they've been to. You don't have to be religious, for example, to sense the peace and love that's often present in a church, or any building that's used for worship. Or go to a nursery school full of happy children busy with creative, playful activities, and feel the joyful atmosphere there. Could it be that some of the "atmosphere" we feel in places like these is due to an angelic presence?

Have you ever visited an ancient building or ruin and felt that you'd suddenly been taken back in time? We can often pick up on the waves of energy that have been created by people who lived in a place long ago. In the same way, we can detect an angelic presence.

If you're ever someplace that feels frightening to you, just call on

41

the angels of light to come and protect you – they can fly in from anywhere!

City Angels, Country Angels

Angels are our doorkeepers. They not only look after us as individuals but they take care of us in a wider sense by helping protect our possessions and surroundings.

That's why there are guardian angels for countries and cities. Think of Los Angeles in California. Its name actually means "City of Angels"! Angels are there, and in every other city in the world, to help protect the city and the people who live and work there. Even if lots of people don't know this consciously, it's interesting that so many towns and cities have statues of angels, as if put there to keep watch.

So even if you don't actually see angels, you may be able to sense their presence. Next time you visit a new place, call on the guardian angel of that place and see if you get any response!

~ ~ Angel Thoughts ~ ~

"An angel flies in the sky and looks like a girl with wings. Some are silver, some are bright. They live in the sky and do jobs for people."

Struan, age 3

"An angel is something that flies into your bedroom when your eyes are closed and gives you kisses."

Harriet, age 4

✧ ✧ ✧

chapter 10

Nighttime and Dreams

It's comforting to know that when we turn out the light at night, our guardian angel will watch over us while we sleep. It's said that at night we are often in touch with our angels even if we aren't aware of it.

Bedside Companions

Angelic messages can come to us in dreams or images, and there are numerous accounts of children who've woken in the night and seen an angel sitting at the foot of their bed. In many of these accounts, the child has had a nightmare or has been thinking the sort of frightening thoughts that turn every nighttime shadow into a monster. At times like this, a bright, shining angel may appear to banish a child's fears.

Here's a very well known prayer that many children say, asking angels to watch over them during the night:

Matthew, Mark, Luke and John,
The bed be blest that I lie on.
Four angels to my bed,

43

Four angels round my head
One to watch, and one to pray,
And two to bear my soul away.[*]

Angelic Night Lights

Have you ever noticed when you're lying in the dark that the room is filled with trillions of tiny white dots? Well, some people say that those dots are the angels of the night! If you ever have problems trying to get to sleep, just tune into the nighttime angels, and chances are you'll be off to dreamland before you know it.

The atmosphere of your bedroom, and how you've decorated it, can have an effect on how you sleep. If you surround yourself with posters of scary monsters, you could well be inviting nightmares. A few pictures of angels, though, would remind you of their protection and would help ease you into a good night's sleep!

The angel Auriel is sometimes called the "overlighting" angel of night. This means that he looks after nighttime as one of his special areas. Auriel is also said to look after the earth, nurturing the seeds in the soil before they come up for light (see Angels of the Seasons in Chapter 16).

[*]This version taken from *In the Charge of an Angel* by Jan Barger (Lion Publishing, 1997).

44

Angel Exercise I

A good tip for guaranteeing a peaceful night is to have a chat with your angels before you drop off to sleep.

If you go to bed with your head full of worries such as unfinished homework or problems with a friend, you'll be burdened with them throughout the night. But if you've talked them over with your angel, you can just release them.

Imagine tying all your problems up in an old sack and handing the sack to your angel, who can put them into an angelic trash can!

Angel Exercise II

If you have a particular problem or worry that you need to resolve, another idea is to write a note to your bedtime angel and put it under your pillow.

By morning you should have a pretty clear idea of what to do. You may even find that the worry has vanished!

Don't forget, the angelic message could come to you through a dream. So keep a notebook and pen beside your bed, and write down any angelic messages or pictures you receive, either during the night or when you wake up in the morning.

Friends in the Dark

Nighttime is an especially good time to contact the angelic realm, because some people say the veil between this world and the next becomes thinner then, and the quiet and stillness of the dark can make it easier for the angels to communicate with us.

Eight-year-old Merrick describes an experience he had just after he'd turned out the light to go to sleep:

"I saw a bright light in the corner of my room. Then it went into the middle of my room and it started to do a figure of eight. Then it moved into every corner and went out through the wall. I know it was the angels visiting me."

A figure eight is a very spiritual symbol, because it has no end, giving us a sense of infinity. It lets us know that there is a part of ourselves, and in fact a part of everything, that lives forever.

Sweet Dreams

Our days are often so hectic and action-packed that it's good to take some time and make some space at bedtime to close the day and move into dream time. Even if you're too tired to have a chat with your guardian angel before you head off into the land of Nod, you can still just call in your angels. Ask them to make sure you have a good night's sleep, and sweet dreams – and you will.

46

~ ~ Angel Thoughts ~ ~

"I see angels as children with wings, who are very kind. They are sort of servants or messengers for God."

Chris, age 11

"Angels have a ring round their head. They have wings, weird names, have harps, and wear little slippers. When my Tamagotchi dies it is an angel!"

Rosie, age 8

chapter 11

Truth

"Truth" is a word that we bandy about fairly easily, often without thinking about what it really means. Of course, as we all know, "telling the truth" can literally mean saying what actually happened rather than making up a story. But there's a deeper meaning, too, all about *living* the truth. In angelic terms it's about living your life with a sense of honor and integrity.

Being True to Yourself

You've probably heard the expression "Be true to yourself." That's what angelic truth is all about – living your life according to your own conscience and sense of rightness. It's not really about being perfect, it's about being in touch with that higher part of yourself that usually knows which path to take, which choice to make, in any situation.

For example, if you believe that you should take more care of your environment, it's not enough just to pay lip service to the idea. Living that truth means putting your ideas and ideals into action. In other words, you would recycle your soda cans and magazines rather than just tossing them in the wastebasket. You'd be careful not to waste water, and you wouldn't ask to be driven places you could safely walk or ride your bike to.

Living your truth also means not saying yes to someone just because you think it will make them feel better. If that "yes" is an untruth for you, in the long run it won't serve any good purpose at all. The truth angels encourage us to be able to speak our truth and live it.

A Step in the Right Direction

In a sense, the angels of truth could be called the angels of conscience. It's easy to do things on impulse, without thinking about the consequences, but our behavior can have a ripple effect on our lives and those of other people. The angels of truth are there to help us take the right steps.

That can mean the difference between cheating on an exam or having the courage to take a stab at the questions even when we're not sure of the answers. Depending on which choice you make, the outcome could be having your exam paper get an automatic failing grade, or getting extra credit for effort.

Truth is the light and hope of humanity. To live a life of deception is the shadow side of truth. On a practical level telling the truth about something we have done usually helps us feel a lot better, whereas fibbing or telling a lie can make us feel uncomfortable inside for a long time. It says in the Bible that "The truth shall make you free." Being honest and living honestly makes us feel great, and the angels are encouraging us all to live this way.

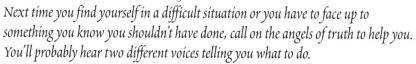

Next time you find yourself in a difficult situation or you have to face up to something you know you shouldn't have done, call on the angels of truth to help you. You'll probably hear two different voices telling you what to do.

The angelic one will be urging you to own up, and assuring you that the consequences of doing so will be much better than what you'll have to face if you cover up and get found out later.

But you might also hear a mischievous little imp encouraging you to lie and try to "get away with it."

Just make sure you turn up the volume of the shiny angel and follow the path of truth – you'll probably be pleasantly surprised at the outcome!

Truth can disarm an angry person far better than an untruth can.

~ ~ Angel Thoughts ~ ~

"An angel is shiny and sprinkles magic dust."

James, age 4

"An angel has wings and a white dress on."

Sedona, age 3

✧ ✧ ✧

chapter 12

Forgiveness

We've already mentioned the angels of love, who are probably among the most important angels for you to be in touch with. That's because love and unity are said to be the foundation of all living things in the universe. But following closely behind the angels of love are the angels of forgiveness. There are plenty of them, because most humans have a few problems in this area! Think about how difficult it can be to forgive ourselves for some of the things we do, let alone trying to forgive others for what we feel they may have done or said against us.

Letting Go

Forgiveness doesn't necessarily produce obvious payoffs, but actually letting go of someone's harmful words or actions really does make you feel better. Holding on to anger and hatred can be far more damaging to us than to the person the bad feelings are directed at. Many spiritual teachers say that being angry at a person is like tying yourself to that person with chains. Forgive them, and the chains are broken. You're free of that individual, and free of your pain.

Treats, with Interest

The angels of forgiveness help us let go of resentments toward other people – and toward ourselves. If it seems too difficult at the time, try to think of each act of forgiveness as money you're putting into a savings account. You know how putting just a little bit in the bank every now and then starts to add up and even earn interest? Before you know it, you've got enough money to buy yourself a really special treat. Well, acts of forgiveness work a little bit like that. You get a big spiritual payoff, with interest, and lots of treats can come your way as a result, even if you don't necessarily know what they're going to be at the time.

Roll Away the Cloud

It's said that every thought we have is a wave of energy that is very real, even if we can't see it. So can you imagine how polluted our planet must be with all the negative thoughts that we put out there. If we could see all that negative energy, it would probably look like an enormous, smelly cloud. But if we all try to love each other a little more and forgive each other for our misdeeds, that ugly cloud will roll away to reveal a bright blue sky.

Even if you can't bring yourself to actually forgive someone, just wanting to can sometimes be enough. Ask the angels of forgiveness to have a word with the other person's guardian angel and miracles will happen. Just wait and see!

~ ~ *Angel Thoughts* ~ ~

"God uses angels to tell people on earth things. They have some of God's power and are bright and shiny. They've got wings but they hardly ever use them – they just appear in places."

Jonathan, age 9

"I think angels are pink, blue, yellow, green, purple, and red. I would like to see one so I can really find out what they do."

Claire, age 5

chapter 13

Pets and Other Animals

*I*t could well be argued that pets are angels on earth. After all, they bring so much pleasure to people. Think of how enjoyable it is to cuddle a rabbit or a kitten, or take an energetic walk with a dog. And think of all the comfort we can get from talking to an animal without being answered back! (Although of course that's not strictly true, because lots of people can communicate with their pets on a psychic level. Have you ever had the feeling, when you're pouring out your problems to your pet, that they really know what you're talking about?)

Our Best Friends?

The most angelic thing about animals is that they are unconditionally loving. Even when we're not so loving toward them, most animals continue to respond lovingly to us (unless, of course, they're treated with real brutality). There seems to be a lot of truth in the phrase "A man's best friend is his dog."

Baby animals are born with all the goodness and purity of angels. If we take care of them in the right way, they continue to behave like that, and they give us so much happiness it's sometimes hard to put it into words.

Some people have reported angels visiting them in the form of animals. There are some truly remarkable stories as well about animals who've saved the lives of humans. It's entirely likely that they were prompted to do so by the angelic realm.

A Human Angel

You may have heard of St. Francis of Assisi, who was visited by angels and adored animals. For his friends in the animal kingdom, St. Francis was an angel in human form. His life showed that our relationship with the angels is not just one-sided. By learning to communicate with angels, we in turn become more angel-like and treat people and animals differently.

Spirit Guides

Many people believe that animals symbolize spiritual and mystical qualities that can help us in our lives. In fact, some Native American tribes believe that each of us has a totem animal as our spirit guide. These totem animals might be whales, dolphins, otters, bears, snakes, or birds, to name but a few.

Animals often possess qualities that can help us in our lives. In some spiritual practices people are asked to go into a meditative state and see which animal appears to them. This is fascinating to do, especially if you want some help in a particular situation. Pick a quiet moment to try it, either on your own or with a friend or member of your family, and see what animal the angels send you.

Angel Exercise

First make sure there are no distractions – no music, TV, or telephones.

Close the door and hang a "Do Not Disturb" sign on it.

Then relax: sit or lie in a comfortable position and empty your head of all its busy thoughts.

When you feel ready, ask for your power animal to appear to you.

Your animal might be a horse, a dog, a leopard, some kind of bird – anything, really. It might come to you in a way you don't expect. You could see it in your mind's eye, or just have a sense of knowing what it is. It really doesn't matter. The most important part of this exercise is to relate to the angelic quality that animal symbolizes.

For example, if you see an eagle, it could mean freedom and the ability to soar above the problems in your life. If a lion comes to you, it might mean strength or courage. A small, fluffy cat could be showing you tenderness.

It's important to remember that your angels are bringing messages for you, not for anyone else, and it's your interpretation that counts. If it feels right to you, it is right.

~ ~ Angel Thoughts ~ ~

"Some are intelligent. They live in heaven, they can be any age, and they are funny. They tell the tooth fairies to give money."

James, age 8

"I've seen a fairy! I think angels look a bit like fairies."

Alice, age 5

✦ ✦ ✦

chapter 14

Nature

Every human being and every creature on the planet has a guardian angel, so it makes sense that every part of the plant and mineral kingdom should have one, too. Angels are the vital link between the invisible and visible worlds, and they hold the blueprint for every living thing.

The Natural Order

If you think about it, the natural world has a perfect order to it. For example, think about a seed. Once it's planted in the ground, it puts roots into the earth, then bursts through the soil into a beautiful flower. Bees can take nectar from this flower and use it to produce honey, which forms part of the human diet.

Mother Earth provides food and shelter for all living beings, and it doesn't all happen accidentally. It really is part of a divine creation, a giant universal plan, and the angels are the team leaders who help ensure that the plan is carried out correctly.

The angels are the ones in overall charge, and in the natural world they have helpers called devas. The devas in turn are helped by "elementals," spirits whose job is to keep peace and harmony.

"Angel Farms"

There are farms and communities in some parts of the world where the devas of plants and trees have made themselves known to humans. Even better, they've given people instructions on how to grow their crops and work in harmony with nature.

One of these communities is Findhorn, in northern Scotland. When it was first set up, Findhorn made headlines because the founders managed to grow magnificent prize-winning fruits and vegetables in soil that everyone else had said was infertile. They claimed they were so successful because they communicated with angels, who told them exactly what to plant, and when and where to plant it.

Green Hope Farm in New Hampshire is another example of how the angels work with nature, using humans as their gardening tools! The gardens are planted in the shapes of symbols that are said to hold special energies that can help bless and heal those who visit them. It's all healing power from the angels!

Essence of Angels

In recent years the idea of flower essences and even angelic essences has become popular. The people who make them say they have direct contact with angels, who help them create the essences. Each essence is said to contain the quality or vibration of that particular flower or angel, which can bring specific benefits to anyone who uses them.

Essences like these are produced at Perelandra, a well-known "angel farm" in Virginia. Its founder, Machaelle Small Wright, works with the devas to grow her healing plants and distill their essences.

Harmony and Peace

"Cooperation" is a key word in describing the way angels and nature work together. Some people say the angels are setting an example for us humans, trying to encourage us to live more harmoniously and lovingly with each other. Nature's forms are perfect, and they can be an inspiration to us humans. When we look at the natural order here on earth, it helps us realize that there is a greater creative force at work, which can also assist us in our lives. The angels are the messengers of that creative force. If magnificent trees and exquisite flowers can grow from tiny seeds planted in the ground, then there's hope for us all!

Some people say that the angelic forces of nature help us see the angelic part of ourselves. It's certainly true that being able to appreciate and work with Mother Earth can make us feel at peace with ourselves and everything around us.

So next time your parents drag you to a garden center, try to think positively – by being around all those plants and flowers, you'll be moving a step or two closer to the angels!

~ ~ Angel Thoughts ~ ~

"They fly in the sky to get in their house, and they're a
bit different from stars. They look like
Power Rangers."

Charlie, age 3

"I think everyone has their own guardian angel, and it looks
like whatever they want it to look like – it's everything they
want it to be."

Skye, age 10

chapter 15

Health

Health is energy, love of life, and working to our full capacity. When we don't have those qualities, we're suffering from ill health.

Those of us who are lucky enough to enjoy good health often take it for granted. We probably don't give a whole lot of thought to our physical bodies. But think about how your life changes when you're not in such good health – if you catch a "bug," for example, or if you sprain your ankle or break an arm. This will give you some idea of how precious a gift a strong, healthy body is.

Inner Health

There's a widely held view that we are what we eat. We are also what we think, and what we feel. In other words, everything we put into our mind, spirit, and body affects our health. You've probably heard the expression "Healthy mind, healthy body."

If you believe your world is bright and beautiful and you enjoy home and school life, then chances are you'll feel energetic and well. If, however, your world seems rather bleak and gray, you might well have a dull, gray complexion, too! You can often tell how someone feels just by looking at his or her eyes. Are they sparkling and shining with health, or are they overcast and dull?

Listening to Your Body

For some people, an illness can symbolize what's wrong in their life. For example, someone who has a sore throat might have something important to say to someone, but it's stuck in his or her throat. If you hurt your leg and end up hobbling along on a pair of crutches, what could that be saying to you? Maybe that you're allowing someone or something to stop you from moving forward freely.

Another way of looking at illness is that it is sometimes a form of cleansing, since it does release toxins from our cells. Often people who've suffered a bereavement or loss become ill; this may be the body's way of releasing the pain.

Some people say that the more ill we get, the more important the message is for us. Illness is like a signpost, telling you that something's wrong somewhere – you're overdoing things, or eating the wrong foods, or not getting enough sleep. If the signpost of illness looms up in your life, look to the angels to show you the right path back to health.

Angelic Healers

We can call on the angels of health at any time, because it's their job to look after our well-being. The chief angel of health and healing is Raphael, also known as "the shining one who heals." In fact, his name actually means "healing of God." Raphael is in charge of lots of angelic helpers who can come to our assistance if we need them. It's said that Raphael works with the elements of air, earth, water, and fire to bring about wholeness and healing for us and the planet.

Helpful Visitors

There are many stories of angels visiting children who are ill. Anastasia first met her angel when she was four years old and was in the hospital for an eye operation. She says she saw an angel that appeared as a wonderful light beside her bed. It talked to her and comforted her. Anastasia said she met the angel again when she went back into the hospital for a second eye operation, and after that had regular encounters with the angelic realm.

Ten-year-old Skye recalls an incident that happened when she was just four years old and traveling with her parents in Indonesia.

"When I was in Bali I cracked my chin open. When they sewed it up I didn't have an anesthetic, and I asked for my guardian angel to look after me. I sang a song that went like this:

I feel better,
I feel better.
I feel fine,
I feel fine.
Yes, I'm feeling better,
Yes, I'm feeling better,
Yes, I'm feeling better.
The pain's gone away.
The pain's gone away.

And I didn't feel a thing."

Angel Exercise

Let's hope you're never ill again, but if you are, and you're stuck in bed feeling sorry for yourself, try this little visualization and see if it speeds up your recovery.

Close your eyes, get your mind into a relaxed space, and call in the angels of health. Ask them to help you to attack the unhealthy cells and give your body a little boost. You can literally imagine winged angels zooming in on the problem cells and zapping them back to good health.

Or imagine the light of the angels pouring through the top of your head and going right through your body and out the soles of your feet. Think of it as pouring a bucket of sunshine over yourself.

You'll probably be amazed at how much better you feel after doing this!

~ ~ *Angel Thoughts* ~ ~

"An angel is a golden ball of light."

Merrick, age 8

"Angels are white with wings, and they have something on top of their heads."

Sarah, age 3

chapter 16

The Calendar

The calendar year is divided up into days, weeks, months, and years. But according to the cycles of nature, the year is divided into the seasons of spring, summer, fall, and winter.

Angels of the Seasons

Each cycle or season has its own guardian angel who oversees particular months and the special qualities that help nature do her work.

Archangel Raphael, known for his healing powers, is in charge of spring, the time of birth.

Archangel Uriel looks after the needs of summer, the time of growth.

Archangel Michael is the angel of the harvest, and so he's in charge of autumn.

And Archangel Gabriel takes care of winter, when things return to the ground.

There are also angels of the four directions or

compass points – north, south, east, and west. And there are angels of the zodiac, who are connected to the time of year when we arrived on this planet. There are angels for days, and given the vast number of celestial helpers around in the universe, there are probably angels assigned to the seconds and minutes that tick by in our day.

Angels of the days

Sunday: **Michael**	Thursday: **Sachiel**
Monday: **Gabriel**	Friday: **Haniel**
Tuesday: **Samael**	Saturday: **Cassiel**
Wednesday: **Raphael**	

Natural Cycles

The angels are a major cog in the wheel of our life. Even if we cannot see them, we can see their presence in the beauty of the world around us and the amazing cycles of nature.

There is a perfection in those cycles that can give us hope that all is well on our planet, even if things do seem turbulent at times! In fact, some say that the violent storms, volcanoes, floods, and fires the world experiences from time to time are simply nature's way of dealing with the negativity on the earth and in us humans.

Part of the angels' job is to teach us to see the bigger picture, to know that just as a flower's purpose is to shoot through the soil and grow toward the sun, there is a purpose and point to our lives here on earth, and that our every thought, word, and action really does matter.

Looking at life as a cycle similar to the cycle of seasons – birth, growth, decay, death, and then rebirth – can help give more meaning to life. It can help us understand that there is a blueprint held by the angels, and that the quality of our life depends on how we live it.

On a practical note, next time you're getting ready to plant seeds in your garden, don't forget to call on the guardian angels of the seasons. They'll be able to give you more than a helping hand!

~ ~ Angel Thoughts ~ ~

"They got told by God to make Jesus alive for three days."

Nathan, age 8

"They are spirits of dead people. They look like fairies and have white and gold clothing."

Parisa, age 10

⁂

chapter 17

Education

*I*n a way, life itself is an education. And there are those who say that this planet we live on is considered the library of the universe, the place to come to learn some real lessons.

Learning and Wisdom

There's a whole host of angels in charge of education and learning, though they would probably call it "wisdom." To most of us, education is about going to school. Wisdom, however, is about becoming wise through life's experiences, no matter what stage of life you're at, from toddler to senior citizen! Although it may be hard to believe sometimes, every experience we go through on earth has a point to it, a higher purpose.

Have you ever noticed how if you make a mistake, the same situation seems to come up again and again? Well, that's the angels making sure that you learn how to overcome a particular difficulty. If you don't get it the first time, you'll definitely find yourself faced with a repeat experience.

Our Sixth Sense

Some people say that we're capable of using more than the five senses of our physical bodies. Besides being able to see, hear, taste, smell, and feel, we have a sixth sense, intuition, with which we can receive all kinds of information. It's through that sense that the angels often send their messages. Have you ever had a thought suddenly pop into your head, or a message of some kind that seems to come from nowhere? Well, that's probably an angel at work.

Look Inside for Answers

It's the angels of wisdom who teach us that what we most need to know is already within ourselves. We can find our own wisdom in a place of quietness inside us, where there is the space for answers and inner knowledge to come to us. Society tells us that teachers know best, but that has to do with what we learn at school. When it comes to knowing what's right for us, the answers are already there.

This doesn't mean that as youngsters we shouldn't look to our parents and teachers for advice and guidance – after all, they've been around for longer than we have! But we all have the potential to access the knowledge and wisdom of the universe.

Wisdom is also about how we use our individual gifts. Some people are terrific at art or music, and others find that math problems are the solution to their life. There are some people who like making things and are good at crafts, while other people seem to possess the common-sense kind of wisdom that can also be helpful to others. It doesn't really matter what form your wisdom takes – what counts is how you use it.

Practical Help

While we're on the subject of education, don't forget that you can always call on the angels of wisdom if you're struggling with a particular piece of schoolwork or have an exam coming up. Exam time can be very stressful, and knowing you have a little extra support can make all the difference.

Sometimes you panic during an exam and though you desperately rummage through your head for the right answer, you come up against a block. If that happens, you can ask your angels to fly down and remind you of all that knowledge packed away in your brain cells. It will definitely take the pressure off!

Aria said she first met the angels when she was a child at school. Her teachers used to think she was deaf because she always seemed so far away, but in fact she was busy connecting with angels and fairies. Aria says her life changed when, as a very young child, she met the Archangel Michael. He appeared to her in a dream and told her about the work she had come to do here on earth. Now, as an adult, Aria works with the angelic realm, helping people connect with their own guardian angels and passing on messages channeled from the angels to those who visit her.

~ ~ *Angel Thoughts* ~ ~

"Grandma's body has gone away, so she can't be an angel –
so she's a fairy instead."

Nathaniel, age 3

"Angels are good spirits that come down and give you
something special when you have done something really
good for someone or something."

Laura, age 11

✧ ✧ ✧

chapter 18

Play

Angels are by their very nature light beings who have an enormous sense of fun and play. They would probably tell us that that's why we're here on earth – to enjoy ourselves and to get as much happiness as possible out of every moment.

Enjoying the Moment

Some people say that just being able to enjoy whatever we're doing right here and now is the real key to happiness. That makes sense when you think about how much time we spend *not* enjoying the present – for example, regretting something we said yesterday, or dreading a history test tomorrow. Being here right now means fully appreciating whatever you're doing at that very moment, whether it's work or play – hanging out with friends or eating dinner with your family, kicking a soccer ball around or doing a science experiment.

Life is built on contrasts and opposites, so of course we have to work to appreciate the moments of play. "Work" can take the form of school lessons, cleaning up after your pet, helping out at home, or having a paper route.

Most adults have to do work of some kind in order to earn a living. But let's be honest – for most of us, the best thing about life is play and leisure time! And wherever there's some fun going on, you can be sure there's an angel winging around nearby.

Laughter *is* the Best Medicine! [or: The Laughter Cure]

The good news is that the most healing activity on earth is laughing! There are even laughter clinics around the world designed to help cure people's illnesses. Laughter is fun, happiness, and joy, and carries the most amazing feel-good factor.

The reason laughter is so vital to our lives is that it has a very healing quality. This is because it moves at a very high frequency.

Everything in the universe is made up of energy, which moves at specific frequencies, or vibratory rates. The higher the frequency, the more healing its vibrations are, and the more easily it moves away from the density of the earth toward the invisible realms of light where the angels live.

You may be able to make sense of this if you think about your moods. How do you feel when you're a little down, or annoyed at something?

Probably sort of heavy and slow-moving. But how do you feel when life's going really well, or you've just achieved something really important, or you're having a great time with your friends? You feel quicker and lighter, don't you? Well that's because when you're in a good mood and enjoying yourself, you are quite literally moving at a different frequency.

Getting the Balance Right

Angels are joyous beings who genuinely want humans to feel a sense of happiness and connectedness with each other. Angels have that sense. They understand that we all come from the same source, and that the only thing that's important in the universe is unconditional love. The more we put into our life, the more we get out of it.

That's why play and leisure time are so important. Play helps give us a sense of balance in our lives. Spending all your time doing schoolwork would make your life seem rather dull and monotonous, wouldn't it? But playing hard and really enjoying your free time balances out all the hard work you do at school.

If you're ever struggling with enjoying yourself, call on the angels of play to get a party going for you. You'll definitely feel better soon.

Angels of Celebrations

Celebrations give us wonderful opportunities to make contact with the angels, and many celebrations have their own overlighting angels. All over the world, in every country and culture, people have come up with wonderful reasons for celebrating. In every faith system, certain days of the year are sacred and are honored with parties or feasts – or sometimes even a fast! (But the fasts almost always end with a big party.)

76

~ ~ Angel Thoughts ~ ~

"An angel is a strange little thing that flies around
in heaven."

Ben, age 8

"An angel can be your guardian angel, and they're in
the Christmas story."

Lucy, age 8

★ ★ ◇

chapter 19

Art and Music

More and more people are coming to believe that everything in the universe is made up of waves of energy that move at different frequencies. Music and art are no exception. Have you ever heard a song or a piece of music that brought tears to your eyes and seemed to touch your very heart? Or maybe you've seen a picture that was so wonderful it gave you a special feeling inside? When something like that happens to us, it's because that particular piece of music or work of art has touched a certain frequency that reminds us of our inner connection to the heart of creation and universal love.

Angelic Inspiration

Records show that people have been drawing and painting angels and gods almost since the beginning of time. Angels represent not just beauty and spirituality, but sort of a safety net between this world and the next. Perhaps that's why artists and composers seem so enchanted by them.

For centuries, angels have been a favorite subject for painters, and some artists have even said they have been angelically inspired. Angels became particularly popular during the Renaissance, when they seemed to adorn almost every available wall and ceiling. And in the late twentieth century, heading toward the millennium, angels are becoming hugely popular again. Gift shops the world over now seem to bulge with angel prints, posters, T-shirts, calendars, and mugs.

Angel Messages

The angels can send us messages through sound and art forms. From angelic cloud shapes in the sky to the tender notes of a violin, our celestial friends are encouraging us to get in touch with the special place inside ourselves.

Angels are beings of brightness and beauty, so it's easy to understand why they might connect with us through songs and pictures. Angels ride on the waves of sound and on the colors of art forms. So the next time you either play or hear a piece of music or sit down at the drawing board, let the angels' messages come through.

Some people say they receive pictures through the angels. There are stories of people who've never been able to draw a stick figure allowing the energy of the angels to come through, then suddenly finding themselves creating stunning works of art.

Angel Exercise

Just for fun, sit down with a blank piece of paper and some crayons or felt-tip pens. Close your eyes, relax, and ask for the angels of creativity to help you make a masterpiece!

In a few moments you might be inspired with a wonderful idea. You might even be able to see a picture in your head that you can reproduce on paper.

If you don't receive any particular image, don't be deterred. Simply get to work and see what happens.

There's no doubt that if you ask for angelic assistance you will be given it; just remember that it arrives in different ways for different people.

No matter what happens, don't be discouraged – whether it's an image, a thought, or a word that comes to you, it's still a signpost from the angelic creative department.

The Joy of Music

If you feel in need of an uplifting mood change, music can be a real help. It can actually change how you feel. If you're feeling sluggish, put on some dance music and get your body moving. You'll definitely feel better at the end of that little exercise. Or if you're feeling stressed out, put on some soothing sounds that will help you relax and put things in perspective. These days there's lots of music around that's designed to help us get into a more meditative state, which can bring real benefits. Some pieces are actually

80

designed to help us connect with the angels. Just having that intention will make good things happen.

> "Music is well said to be the speech of angels."
> Thomas Carlyle

~ ~ Angel Thoughts ~ ~

"Angels are people that were good when they were alive.
They normally wear white because it is the color of light.
Angels normally carry small instruments called lyres."

James, age 8

"An angel is one of God's messengers. There is a difference between
angels and ghosts. An angel looks the same as another angel.
All ghosts are different. They look more like humans. Ghosts
only come back if they have unfinished business on earth.
Angels come from heaven."

Sarah, age 10

★ ★ ✧

Chapter 20

Communication

"Communication" is one of the most vital words in our language today, but we don't always stop to think about its true significance. Communication is one of our key tools for living and for making this world a better place. Whether it's through speech, body language, eye contact, or what's known as our sixth sense or intuition, giving and receiving messages is essential to the lives of humans, animals, and even plants.

A Tool for Survival

From the moment we're born we need to communicate in order to survive. A newborn baby can't talk, but it can tell its mother it's hungry through sounds. As it gets older, a child learns to ask for what it wants – in fact, there's an expression that some people use: "If you don't ask, you don't get."

A bee knows which flower to gather nectar from because that flower communicates to the bee by giving off a certain smell that the bee recognizes. We speak, we write, we draw, we compose music, we make films – the list of ways we communicate is almost endless. So it's vital that we get in touch with our communication angels when we have something important to say.

Good News

The Archangel Gabriel is probably the angel best known for his communication skills. He was the messenger who brought Mary the news that she would give birth to Jesus,  and he was said to be the guardian angel of the Muslim prophet Muhammad. He is also known as the angel who helps interpret dreams. Gabriel brings good news and messages of truth and love, and he is the leader of a large band of angels who are here to help us humans learn to communicate better with one another.

The Words of Angels

Have you ever found yourself in this situation? Someone has asked you for advice, and even though you're not really sure what to say, you suddenly hear exactly the right words coming out of your mouth – almost as if someone else were speaking? Sometimes if our speech is inspired or seems to contain a meaning that surprises even ourselves, it's a pretty good bet that an angel's at work! That can happen on a regular basis if you just remember to tune into the angel of communication and ask for a little help.

In any situation, if you want to say or write something and you need to be very clear about it, ask for some winged wisdom. The angels are very close by, just waiting to be called on.

Good Vibrations

Words, like everything else in the universe, are made up of energy, and each one holds a particular vibration or travels at a certain frequency. So it's especially important that we speak, write, sing, and so on with a sense of love, honor, and integrity. That may not always be easy. If we're upset about something, for example, it can be hard to say exactly what we mean. Or if we're nervous, maybe about speaking in front of an audience, we might feel as if we're about to freeze up. In situations like these, the angels of communication are ready to help. You just have to remember to call on them.

Anytime you're anxious about communicating with anyone, imagine Gabriel and his band giving you an angel's golden trumpet to speak through – you'll never have to worry about how you're coming across again.

~ ~ Angel Thoughts ~ ~

"Angels have wings and live in heaven. They have halos on their heads. They are very nice and sit on the clouds and play the harp."

Sean, age 9

"Angels look like anybody else, but they can fly and have light glowing out of them. They help people if they are ill or sad."

Beth, age 11

chapter 21

Being an Angel

*I*t's said that there are angels disguised as human beings.

The angelic realm is a bridge between this world and the invisible realms, with the angels acting as a sort of footpath to the source of creation. Some angel experts believe that there are beings who've chosen to live on earth as humans in order to help people get in touch with the angelic part of themselves. There are also a growing number of stories about people who've been rescued by so-called humans who suddenly appear on the scene in the middle of a crisis, do their bit, and then vanish into thin air. Miracles? Or angels?

The Angel Inside Us

Miracles aside, one of the purposes of being here on earth is to see the angel in ourselves and others, and we can start doing that by being kind and considerate. It's also important to be good to ourselves and to appreciate our own efforts and achievements. No matter what our individual beliefs or cultural background might be, most of us would agree that we're likely to get more out of life by behaving like an angel rather than a rascal!

Accentuate the Positive

Angelic qualities are love, truth, peace, joy, and wisdom – in other words, all the qualities that are light and positive. It's a great help to know that for every negative quality you come up against, there is always an opposite positive to replace it. For example, if you feel frightened about something try replacing your fear with faith, or belief in something positive that has more power than the worry on your mind.

There are other obvious opposites, such as replacing hate with love, jealousy with generosity, loss with gain, sorrow with joy. The list goes on. The important thing to remember is that our thoughts become reality. So the more positive we are in our heads, the more likely we are to lead positive and fulfilling lives.

Of course, it's easy enough to say all this, but sometimes it's really hard to act this way on our own. Our brain cells love to get busy with all sorts of imaginary fears and worries about what might happen in the future. That's where our angels come in. If in doubt, call on one for a bit of help.

Acting Like Angels

Angels can also help us behave more like angels. Next time you find yourself in a situation where you could be either angelic or mischievous, call on the angels to help you act from your heart rather than your head.

It's easy for us to think that what we do or even think can go unseen, but of course that's not true. Those overlighting angels are flying around, well aware of what we're up to, and they will definitely reward us for good behavior!

The angels' message is very simple: open your heart, be loving and giving, and you will receive many gifts in return. If we all try to act a little more like angels in our everyday lives, who knows what miracles we can bring about!

"Always be an angel on call for a friend."*

~ ~ Angel Thoughts ~ ~

"Angels are sort of God's assistants. They might not necessarily be good."

Daniel, age 11

"I've seen the film *Angels*, where a boy meets some. They dressed in white clothes with a gold collar and a silver crown."

Florence, age 8

*Taken from *Angels are Forever* (Peter Pauper Press, 1994).

chapter 22

Family and Community

Probably one of the best things about being alive is belonging to a family of some kind. No matter where we come from, or how we live, on some level we are part of some sort of community. And within that community, we belong to a family. Even if you don't live in a conventional family situation, if you are living with others, you are part of a group or family.

A Protective Wing

Besides guardian angels for each soul, there are angels keeping a protective wing over families and communities. There's nothing the angels like more than to see the love and joy that come from people sharing with one another – giving and receiving love, taking care of each other, and just going about the ordinary business of living.

Angels are here to help us see the angelic or special divine qualities in each other. In the busy, stressed-out lives so many of us lead, it's too easy to lose sight of those divine qualities. But making the space to spend some time with our families strengthens the foundations of our lives and helps build up the love.

In a family, it's sometimes the small things we do together that can mean the most. Going for a walk, sharing a meal, even doing the dishes! They can all be great times for good conversations, unloading some of our worries, chewing over problems, and sharing our happiness. It's those times that help us remember that we are human after all, and that's something we all have in common.

Getting Together

The angels of families are also eager to help out on team sports or pastimes that involve people getting together and sharing. A sense of camaraderie, the joy of winning, and the group support when we lose are all part of being in a team. All those situations can not only help us lead enjoyable and fulfilled lives, but they also play a real part in helping us live in a more angelic way.

The angels of families help us appreciate ourselves and those around us. When you see how happy you can make your parents by doing what they ask you to, or how grateful your brother or sister is when you share one of your prized possessions, it can make you feel pretty good.

Tolerance, patience, love, and kindness are definitely attributes we have to work on, and the family angels are right there to support us in doing that.

~ ~ *Angel Thoughts* ~ ~

"They bring messages and come from heaven."

Johanna, age 8

"Angels are meant to glow!"

Leigh-Anne, age 9

✧ ✧ ✧

chapter 23

Gratitude

I t's easy to think that gratitude is just being polite and saying thank you for things you are given. But that's only one aspect of gratitude. Gratitude in the angelic sense is feeling appreciation for the good things in our lives, and also being thankful for situations in which we can learn and grow.

Challenging Experiences

The angels of gratitude teach us that it's sometimes the experiences that make us the most uncomfortable that are the ones we later look back on and see as real turning points in our lives. It's said that we are given lessons to learn over and over again until we "get them" and can move on to the next stage. If there's a challenging situation that keeps coming up in your life, try looking at it differently next time, and see whether reacting in another way might change things.

Appreciating Our Lives

It can be easy to focus on what's not working in our lives – moaning about how boring school's getting, wishing we could go on vacations that our family can't afford, or constantly waiting for the future rather than enjoying the present. The angels of gratitude helps us enjoy the moment and appreciate our friends and family right now.

Next time you feel irritated with one of your friends, try switching that negative thought to a positive one by appreciating something good about that person. You'll probably find that leads to a sense of gratitude for his or her friendship, and the irritating thought will have completely disappeared.

Give and Take

For the world to be balanced, we have to have the polarities of light and dark, positive and negative. Our lives are like that, too. We can only truly experience gratitude for things or people if we know what it's like not to have them in our lives. Next time you're feeling annoyed with your parents, imagine what it would be like if they weren't around to love and look after you (not to mention to act as your personal taxi service!).

Gratitude is appreciation of what we have and valuing what exists at the moment. It's also about sharing and putting something into life so that we can get something out of it. Life, like relationships, can't work if it's one-way only. Taking without giving would become hollow and meaningless for us after a while, whereas knowing that we've made a contribution can give us a sense of gratitude as well.

Silver Linings

Calling on the gratitude angels will help us find positive solutions to seemingly impossible problems, and will help us release any resentments or anger and frustration we might feel about something. Most of all, getting in touch with the angels of gratitude will help us open our hearts and really feel good about the people and situations in our lives.

The angels are the silver linings to the clouds because they help us see the highest good in every moment.

~ ~ Angel Thoughts ~ ~

Her gilded wings are feather light,
Her radiance transcending through the night,
Vanquishing my fears of life,
Showering my path with a guiding light.
She gives me strength to carry on
My journey to the break of dawn.

by Traian Tulbure, age 11

Bibliography

Angel Energy: How to Harness the Power of Angels in Your Everyday Life, by John Randolph Price (New York: Ballantine Books, 1995).

Angels and Mortals, by Maria Parisen (Wheaton, Illinois: Quest Books, 1991).

Angels Are Forever (New York: Peter Pauper Press, 1994).

Angels: An Endangered Species, by Malcolm Godwin (London: Boxtree Ltd., 1993).

A Dictionary of Angels, by Gustav Davidson (New York: Free Press / Macmillan, 1994).

Encyclopedia of Angels, by Rosemary Ellen Guiley (New York: Facts on File, 1996).

In the Charge of an Angel, by Jan Barger (Oxford: Lion Publishing, 1997).

Meetings with Angels, by Dr. H. C. Moolenburgh (Saffron Walden, England: The C. W. Daniel Company Ltd., 1992).

Messengers of Light: The Angels' Guide to Spiritual Growth, by Terry Lynn Taylor (Tiburon, California: H. J. Kramer, Inc., 1990).

The Sacred Magic of the Angels, by David Goddard (York Beach, Maine: Samuel Weiser, Inc., 1996).

Acknowledgments

It has been a real pleasure to write this book and I know there were several angels at my shoulder helping it along! I would also like to thank Element Children's Books Director Barry Cunningham and Editor Ronne Randall who were great to work with. My gratitude also goes to June Ferguson, Mandy Falkus, Hilary Walsh, the pupils of Newbridge Junior School in Bath, England, and all the children who told me about their angelic experiences.